Why Did
Jesus D

Booklets taken from Questions of Life:

Is There More to Life Than This?

Who Is Jesus?

Why Did Jesus Die?

How Can We Have Faith?

Why and How Do I Pray?

Why and How Should I Read the Bible?

How Does God Guide Us?

The Holy Spirit

How Can I Resist Evil?

Why and How Should I Tell Others?

Does God Heal Today?

What About the Church?

How Can I Make the Most of the Rest of My Life?

Why Did Jesus Die?

NICKY GUMBEL

ISBN: 978 1 909309 59 3

Published by Alpha International
Holy Trinity Brompton
Brompton Road
London SW7 1JA
Email:
internationalpublishing@alpha.org

Illustrated by Charlie Mackesy

Contents

Why Did Jesus Die?

What do Madonna, Elton John, Bono and the Pope have in common? One answer is that they all wear a cross. Many people today go around with a cross on their earrings, bracelet or necklace or even etched on their body as a tattoo. We are so used to seeing this we are not shocked by it. But we might be shocked if we saw someone wearing a gallows or an electric chair round their neck, and the cross was just as much a form of execution. Indeed, it was one of the cruellest forms of execution known to humankind. It was abolished in AD 337 because ultimately even the Romans considered it too inhumane.

" umm.. They all have "O" in their names? "

Yet the cross has always been regarded as the symbol of the Christian faith. A high proportion of the Gospels is about the death of Jesus. Much of the rest of the New Testament is concerned with explaining what happened on the cross – why Jesus died. The central service of the church, the Communion service, focuses on the broken body and shed blood of Jesus. Churches are often built in the shape of a cross. When the apostle Paul went to Corinth he said, 'I resolved to know nothing while I was with you except Jesus Christ and him crucified' (1 Corinthians 2:2). Most leaders who have influenced nations or even changed the world are remembered for the impact of their lives. Jesus, who more than any other person changed the face of world history, is remembered for his death even more than for his life.

Why is there such concentration on the death of Jesus? What is the difference between his death and the death of Socrates, or one of the martyrs, or of a war hero? What did it achieve? What does it mean when the New Testament says he died 'for our sins'? Why did he die for our sins? The answer in a nutshell is 'because God loves you'. Raniero Cantalamessa, Preacher to the Papal Household, said, 'The love of God is the answer to all the "whys" in the Bible: the why of creation, the why of the incarnation, the why of redemption.'[1] It is because 'God so loved the world' that he sent his one and only Son to die for us so that 'whoever believes in him shall not perish but have eternal life' (John 3:16).

The problem

Sometimes people say, 'I have no need for Christianity.' They say something along the lines of, 'I am quite happy, my life is full and I try to be nice to other people and lead a good life.' According to the Bible, every human being is created in the image of God. There is therefore something good and noble about every person. This understanding of human nature has been a tremendous force for good in world history. In fact, it has laid the foundations for our modern understanding of human dignity and human rights by insisting that we are more than just bundles of genes and products of our environment. There is, however, a flip side to the coin. Certainly in my own life I would have to admit there are things I do that I know are wrong – I make mistakes. In order to understand why Jesus died we have to go back and look at the greatest problem that confronts every person.

If we are honest, we would all have to admit that we do things we know are wrong. Paul wrote: 'All have sinned and fall short of the glory of God' (Romans 3:23). In other words, relative to God's standards we all fall a long way short. If we compare ourselves to armed robbers or child molesters or even our neighbours, we may think we come off quite well. But when we compare ourselves to Jesus Christ, we see how far short we fall. Playwright and novelist Somerset Maugham once said, 'If I wrote down every thought I have ever thought and every deed I have ever done, men would call me a monster of depravity.'[2]

The essence of sin is rebellion against God – our ignoring God in the sense of behaving as if he does not exist (Genesis 3), or choosing to do things that are wrong; with the result that we are cut off from him. Like the prodigal son (Luke 15), we find ourselves far from our Father's home having made a mess of our lives. Sometimes people say, 'If we are all in the same boat, does it really matter?' The answer is that it does matter because of the consequences of sin. These can be summarised under four headings.

The pollution of sin

Jesus said that it is possible for us to pollute the lives God has given us. Jesus said, 'What comes out of you is what makes you "unclean". For from within, out of your hearts, come evil thoughts, sexual immorality, theft, murder, adultery, greed, malice, deceit, lewdness, envy, slander, arrogance and folly. All these evils come from inside and make you "unclean"' (Mark 7:20–23). These things pollute our lives.

You may say, 'I do not do most of these things.' But one of them alone is enough to mess up our lives. We might wish the Ten Commandments were like an examination paper in which we only have to 'attempt any three' of them. But the New Testament says that if we break *any* part of the law we are guilty of breaking all of it (James 2:10). It is not possible, for example, to have a 'reasonably clean' driving licence. Either it is clean or it is not. One driving offence stops it from being a clean licence. So it is with us; one offence makes our lives unclean.

The power of sin

The things we do wrong often have an addictive power. Jesus said, 'Everyone who sins is a slave to sin' (John 8:34). It is easier to see this in some areas of our wrongdoing than in others. For example, it is well known that if someone takes a hard drug like heroin, it soon becomes an addiction.

It is also possible to be addicted to bad temper, envy, arrogance, pride, selfishness, slander or sexual immorality. These things can take hold of our lives. We can become addicted to patterns of thought or behaviour which, on our own, we cannot break. This is the slavery which Jesus spoke about. This is what has such a destructive power over our lives.

Bishop J. C. Ryle, a former bishop of Liverpool, once wrote:

> Each and all [sins] have crowds of unhappy
> prisoners bound hand and foot in their chains...
> The wretched prisoners... boast sometimes
> that they are eminently free... There is no
> slavery like this. Sin is indeed the hardest of all
> task-masters. Misery and disappointment by
> the way, despair and hell in the end – these are
> the only wages that sin pays to its servants.[3]

The penalty for sin

There is something in human nature which cries out
for justice. When we hear of children being molested
or old people being attacked brutally in their homes,
we long for the people who have done these things to
be caught and punished. We believe there should be a
penalty. Often our motives may be mixed: there may
be an element of revenge as well as a desire for justice.
But there is such a thing as justified anger. We are right
to feel that sins should be punished and that people
who do such things should not get away with them.

It is not just other people's sins that deserve
punishment; it is our own as well. One day we will all
be subject to the judgment of God. St Paul tells us that
'the wages of sin is death' (Romans 6:23).

The partition of sin

The death Paul speaks of is not only physical. It is
a spiritual death, which results in eternal isolation

from God. This cutting off from God begins now. The prophet Isaiah proclaimed, 'Surely the arm of the Lord is not too short to save, nor his ear too dull to hear. But your iniquities have separated you from your God; your sins have hidden his face from you, so that he will not hear' (Isaiah 59:1–2). The things we do wrong cause this barrier. It is similar to when we fall out with someone and we cannot look them in the eye. There is something between us. Sometimes people say, 'I've tried praying but my prayers seem to hit the ceiling.' There is a partition: the things we do wrong have built a barrier between us and God.

The solution

We all need to deal with the problem of sin in our lives. The greater our understanding of our need the more we will appreciate what God has done. The good news of Christianity is that God loves us and he did not leave us in the mess that we make of our own lives.

In the person of his Son, Jesus, God came to Earth to die instead of us (2 Corinthians 5:21; Galatians 3:13). This has been called the 'self-substitution of God'.[4] In the words of the apostle Peter, '*He* himself bore *our* sins in *his* body on the tree... by *his* wounds you have been healed' (1 Peter 2:24, italics mine).

On the last day of July 1941 the sirens of Auschwitz announced the escape of a prisoner from Block 14. As a reprisal, ten of his fellow prisoners would die – a long, slow starvation, buried alive in a purpose-built, concrete bunker. All day, tortured by heat-stroke, hunger and fear, the men waited in the courtyard as the German commandant and his SS assistant walked between the ranks to select, quite arbitrarily, the chosen ten. As the commandant pointed to one man, Franciszek Gajowniczek, he cried out in despair, 'My wife! My children.' At that moment the unimpressive figure of a man with sunken eyes and round glasses in wire frames stepped out of line and took off his cap.

'I am a Catholic priest; I want to die for that man. I am old, he has a wife and children... I have no one,' said Father Maximilian Kolbe.

'Request granted,' retorted the commandant, before moving on.

That night, nine men and one priest went to the starvation bunker. Normally they would tear each other apart like cannibals. Not so this time. While they had strength, lying naked on the floor, the men prayed and sang psalms. After two weeks, two of the men and Father Maximilian were still alive. The bunker was required for others, so on 14 August, the remaining three were disposed of. At 12.50 pm, after two weeks in the starvation bunker and still conscious, the Polish priest was finally given an injection of carbolic acid and died at the age of forty-seven.

On 10 October 1982 in St Peter's Square, Rome, Father Maximilian's death was put in its proper perspective. Present in the crowd of 150,000, including twenty-six cardinals and 300 bishops and archbishops, was Francis Gajowniczek and his family – for indeed, many had been saved by that one man. The Pope, describing Father Maximilian's death, said, 'This was a victory won over all the systems of contempt and hate in man – a victory like that won by our Lord Jesus Christ.'

When Francis Gajowniczek died, aged ninety-four, I read his obituary in *The Independent*. He had spent the rest of his life going around telling people what Maximilian Kolbe had done for him, dying in his place. Jesus' death was even more amazing because it was not just for one man, but for every single person in the world.

Jesus came as our substitute. He endured crucifixion for us. Roman statesman Cicero described crucifixion as 'the most cruel and hideous of tortures'. Jesus was stripped and tied to a whipping post. He was flogged with four or five thongs of leather interwoven with sharp jagged bone and lead. Eusebius, the third-century church historian, described Roman flogging in these terms: the sufferer's 'veins were laid bare, and... the very muscles, sinews and bowels of the victim were open to exposure'. He was then taken to Pilate's headquarters where a crown of thorns was thrust onto his head. He was mocked by a battalion of about 600 men and hit about the face and head. He was then forced to carry a heavy cross bar on his bleeding shoulders until he collapsed, and Simon of Cyrene was press-ganged into carrying it for him.

When they reached the site of crucifixion, he was again stripped naked. He was laid on the cross, and six-inch nails were driven into his forearms, just above the wrist. His knees were twisted sideways so that the ankles could be nailed between the tibia and the Achilles' tendon. He was lifted up on the cross which was then dropped into a socket in the ground. There he was left to hang in intense heat and unbearable thirst, exposed to the ridicule of the crowd. He hung there in unthinkable pain for six hours while his life slowly drained away. It was the height of pain and the depth of shame.

Yet the worst part of his suffering was not the physical agony of torture and crucifixion, nor even the emotional pain of being rejected by the world and deserted by his friends, but the spiritual agony, cut off from his Father as he carried our sins.

Jesus' victory was total – he died not just for one person but for all of us – and it was also costly. In all four Gospels, we hear of Jesus' agony in the Garden of Gethsemane, alone, crying out to his Father, 'Abba,

Father... Take this cup from me. Yet not what I will, but what you will' (Mark 14:36).

Raniero Cantalamessa writes:

> In the Bible the image of the cup almost always evokes the idea of God's wrath against sin... Wherever sin exists, God's judgment cannot but be focussed on it, otherwise God would reach a compromise with sin and the very distinction itself between good and evil would no longer exist. Now, Jesus... is... man 'made sin'. Christ, it is written, died 'for sinners'; he died in their place and not only in their favour... he is, therefore, 'responsible' for all, the guilty one before God! It is against him that God's wrath is 'revealed' and that is what 'drinking the cup' means.[5]

The result

The cross is like a beautiful diamond, with many facets. From whichever angle you look at it you can see different colours and lights. The cross in a sense is a mystery; it is something too profound for understanding. However, from whichever angle you look at the cross you will never fathom its full depth and beauty. In the New Testament these angles are explored.

First, the cross shows just how much God loves us. If you are ever in any doubt that God loves us, look at the cross. Jesus said, 'Greater love has no one than this, to lay down one's life for one's friends' (John 15:13). The cross also tells us something about the nature of God. Probably the biggest question people ask about Christianity is: How can God allow so much suffering in the world? There are no simple answers to this difficult question but we do know this: God himself is not aloof from suffering. He has come in the person of his Son, he suffered for us, and he now suffers alongside us. On the cross Jesus sets us an example of self-sacrificial love (1 Peter 2:21). The cross and the resurrection, which are in a sense one event, tell us that the powers of death and evil have been defeated (Colossians 2:15).

Each of these aspects deserves a chapter of its own, which space does not allow. However, I do want to concentrate here on four images that the New Testament uses to describe what Jesus did on the cross for us.[6] As John Stott, well-known author and former Rector Emeritus of All Souls, Langham Place, London, pointed out, each of them is taken from a different area of day-to-day life.

The first image comes from the *temple*. In the Old Testament, very careful laws were laid down as to how sins should be dealt with. There was a whole system of sacrifices which demonstrated the seriousness of sin and the need for cleansing from it.

In a typical case the sinner would take an animal. The animal was to be as near perfection as possible. The sinner would lay his hands on the animal and confess his sins. Thus the sins were seen to pass from the sinner to the animal which was then killed.

The writer of Hebrews points out that it is 'impossible for the blood of bulls and goats to take away sins' (Hebrews 10:4). It was only a picture or a 'shadow' (Hebrews 10:1). The reality came with the sacrifice of Jesus. Only the blood of Christ, our substitute, can take away our sin. When John the Baptist saw Jesus he said 'Look, the Lamb of God, who takes away the sin of the world!' (John 1:29). He alone was the perfect sacrifice since he alone lived a perfect life. Jesus' blood purifies us from all sin (1 John 1:7). It washes away and removes *the pollution of sin*.

The second image comes from the *market-place*. Debt is not a problem confined to the present day; it was a problem in the ancient world as well. If someone had serious debts, he might be forced to sell himself into slavery in order to pay them off. Suppose a man was standing in the market-place, offering himself as a slave. Someone might have pity on him and ask, 'How much do you owe?' The debtor might say, '10,000.' Suppose the customer offers to pay the 10,000 and then lets him go free. In doing so, he would be 'redeeming him' by paying a 'ransom price'. In a similar way for us 'redemption... came by Jesus Christ' (Romans 3:24).

Jesus by his death on the cross paid the ransom price (Mark 10:45).

In this way, we are set free from the power of sin. This is true freedom. Jesus said, 'If the Son sets you free, you will be free indeed' (John 8:36). When I became a Christian I was instantly set free from some things, but in other areas it has been a continual struggle. It is not that we never sin again, but that sin's hold over us is broken.

Billy Nolan ran away from the merchant navy and was an alcoholic for thirty-eight years. For twenty years he sat outside HTB Brompton Road, our church, drinking alcohol and begging for money. On 13 May 1990 he looked in the mirror and said to himself, 'You're not the Billy Nolan I once knew.' To use his own expression, he asked the Lord Jesus Christ into his life and made a covenant with him that he would never drink alcohol again. He has not touched a drop since. His life is transformed. He radiates the love and joy of Christ. I once said to him, 'Billy, you look happy.' He replied, 'I am happy because I am free. Life is like a maze and at last I have found a way out through Jesus Christ.' Jesus' death on the cross made this freedom from *the power of sin* possible.

The third image comes from the *law court*. Paul says that through Christ's death 'we have been justified' (Romans 5:1). Justification is a legal term. If you went to court and were acquitted, you were justified. There is one illustration that particularly helped me to understand what this means.

Two people went through school and university together and developed a close friendship. Life went on and they went their different ways and lost contact. One went on to become a judge, while the other one went down and down and ended up a criminal. One day the criminal appeared before the judge. He had committed a crime to which he pleaded guilty. The judge recognised his old friend, and faced a dilemma. He was a judge so he had to be just; he couldn't let the man off. On the other hand, he didn't want to punish the man, because he loved him. So he told his friend that he would fine him the correct penalty for the offence. That is justice. Then he came down from his position as judge and he wrote a cheque for the amount of the fine. He gave it to his friend, saying that he would pay the penalty for him. That is love.

This is an illustration of what God has done for us. In his justice, he judges us because we are guilty, but then, in his love, he came down in the person of his Son Jesus Christ and paid the penalty for us. In this way he is both 'just' (in that he does not allow the guilty to go unpunished) and 'the one who justifies' – Romans 3:26 (in that by taking the penalty himself, in the person of his Son, he enables us to go free). He is both our Judge and our Saviour. It is not an innocent third party but God himself who saves us. In effect, he gives us a cheque and says we have a choice: do we want him to pay it for us or are we going to face the judgment of God for our own wrongdoing?

The illustration I have used is not an exact one for three reasons. First, our plight is worse. The penalty we are facing is not just a fine, but death. Second, the relationship is closer. This is not just two friends: it is our Father in heaven who loves us more than any earthly parent loves their own child. Third, the cost was greater: it cost God not money, but his one and only Son – who paid *the penalty of sin*.

The fourth image comes from the *home*. We saw that both the root and the result of sin were a broken relationship with God. The result of the cross is the possibility of a restored relationship with God. Paul says that '*God was* reconciling the world to himself *in Christ*' (2 Corinthians 5:19, italics mine). Some people caricature the New Testament teaching and suggest that God is barbaric and unjust because he punished Jesus, an innocent party, instead of us. This is not what the New Testament says. Rather, Paul says, 'God was... in Christ.' He was himself the substitute in the person of his Son. He made it possible for us to be restored to a relationship with him. The *partition of sin* has been destroyed; 'the curtain of the temple was torn in two from top to bottom' (Matthew 27:51).

What happened to the prodigal son can happen to us. We can come back to the Father and experience his love and blessing. The relationship is not only for this life: it is eternal. One day we will be with the Father in a heaven and earth made new – there we will be free, not only from the penalty of sin, the power of sin, the pollution of sin and the partition of sin, but also from the presence of sin. That is what God has made possible through his self-substitution on the cross.

God loves each one of us so much and longs to be in a relationship with us as a human parent longs to be in a relationship with each of their children. It is not just that Jesus died for everyone. He died for you and for me; it is intensely personal. Paul writes of 'the Son of God, who loved me and gave himself for me' (Galatians 2:20). If you had been the only person in the world, Jesus would have died for you. As St Augustine put it, 'he died for every one of us as if there were only one of us'. Once we see the cross in these personal terms, our lives will be transformed.

John Wimber, an American pastor and church leader, described how the cross became a personal reality to him:

> After I had studied the Bible for about three months I could have passed an elementary exam on the cross. I understood there is one God who could be known in three Persons. I understood Jesus is fully God and fully man and he died on the cross for the sins of the world. But I didn't understand that I was a sinner. I thought I was a good guy. I knew I messed up here and there but I didn't realise how serious my condition was.
>
> But one evening around this time Carol [his wife] said, 'I think it's time to do something about all that we've been learning.' Then, as I looked on in utter amazement, she knelt down on the floor and started praying to what seemed to me to be the ceiling plaster. 'Oh God,' she said, 'I am sorry for my sin.'
>
> I couldn't believe it. Carol was a better person than I, yet she thought she was a sinner. I could feel her pain and the depth of her prayers. Soon she was weeping and repeating, 'I am sorry for my sin.' There were six or seven people in the room, all with their eyes closed. I looked at them and then it hit me: *They've*

all prayed this prayer too! I started sweating bullets. I thought I was going to die. The perspiration ran down my face and I thought, 'I'm not going to do this. This is dumb. I'm a good guy.' Then it struck me. Carol wasn't praying to the plaster; she was praying to a person, to a God who could hear her. In comparison to him she knew she was a sinner in need of forgiveness.

In a flash the cross made personal sense to me. Suddenly I knew something that I had never known before; I had hurt God's feelings. He loved me and in his love for me he sent Jesus. But I had turned away from that love; I had shunned it all of my life. I was a sinner, desperately in need of the cross.

Then I too was kneeling on the floor, sobbing, nose running, eyes watering, every square inch of my flesh perspiring profusely. I had this overwhelming sense that I was talking with someone who had been with me all of my life, but whom I failed to recognise. Like Carol, I began talking to the living God, telling him that I was a sinner but the only words I could say aloud were, 'Oh God, oh God.'

I knew something revolutionary was going on inside of me. I thought, 'I hope this works, because I'm making a complete fool of myself.'

Then the Lord brought to mind a man I had seen in Pershing Square in Los Angeles a number of years before. He was wearing a sign that said, 'I'm a fool for Christ. Whose fool are you?' I thought at the time, 'That's the most stupid thing I've ever seen.' But as I kneeled on the floor I realised the truth of the odd sign: the cross is foolishness 'to those who are perishing' (1 Corinthians 1:18). That night I knelt at the cross and believed in Jesus. I've been a fool for Christ ever since.[7]

Endnotes

1. Raniero Cantalamessa, *Life in Christ* (Vineyard Publishing, 1997), p.7.
2. Jeffrey Myers, *Somerset Maugham* (University of Michigan Press, 2004), p.347.
3. Bishop J. C. Ryle, *Expository Thoughts on the Gospel*, Vol. III, John 1:1–John 10:30 (Evangelical Press, 1977).
4. John Stott, *The Cross of Christ* (IVP, 1996). See also Catechism of the Catholic Church, chapter 2, line 444, paragraph 615, entitled: 'Jesus substitutes his obedience for our disobedience'. By his obedience unto death, Jesus accomplished the substitution of the suffering Servant, who 'makes himself an offering for sin', when 'he bore the sin of many', and who 'shall make many to be accounted righteous', for 'he shall bear their iniquities'.
5. Raniero Cantalamessa, *Life in Christ* (Vineyard Publishing, 1997), pp.52–53.
6. We deal with religious concepts using metaphors and parables. For the atonement there is no one seminal metaphor, no one all-encompassing parable. All are approximations, which, like the radii of a circle, converge on the same central point without ever quite touching it.
7. John Wimber, *Equipping the Saints*, Vol. 2, No. 2, Spring 1988 (Vineyard Ministries, 1988).

Alpha

Alpha is a practical introduction to the Christian faith, initiated by HTB in London and now being run by thousands of churches, of many denominations, throughout the world. If you are interested in finding out more about the Christian faith and would like details of your nearest Alpha, please visit our website:

alpha.org

or contact:
The Alpha Office,
HTB Brompton Road,
London,
SW7 1JA

Tel: 0845 644 7544

Alpha titles available

Why Jesus? A booklet – given to all participants at the start of Alpha. 'The clearest, best illustrated and most challenging short presentation of Jesus that I know.' – Michael Green

Why Christmas? The Christmas version of *Why Jesus?*

Questions of Life Alpha in book form. In fifteen compelling chapters Nicky Gumbel points the way to an authentic Christianity which is exciting and relevant to today's world.

Searching Issues The seven issues most often raised by participants on Alpha, including, suffering, other religions, science and Christianity, and the Trinity.

A Life Worth Living What happens after Alpha? Based on the book of Philippians, this is an invaluable next step for those who have just completed Alpha, and for anyone eager to put their faith on a firm biblical footing.

The Jesus Lifestyle   Studies in the Sermon on the Mount showing how Jesus' teaching flies in the face of a modern lifestyle and presents us with a radical alternative.

30 Days   Nicky Gumbel selects thirty passages from the Old and New Testament which can be read over thirty days. It is designed for those on Alpha and others who are interested in beginning to explore the Bible.

All titles are by Nicky Gumbel,
who is vicar of Holy Trinity Brompton

About the Author

Nicky Gumbel is the pioneer of Alpha. He read law at Cambridge and theology at Oxford, practised as a barrister and is now vicar of HTB in London. He is the author of many bestselling books about the Christian faith, including *Questions of Life*, *The Jesus Lifestyle*, *Why Jesus?*, *A Life Worth Living*, *Searching Issues* and *30 Days*.

Lightning Source UK Ltd.
Milton Keynes UK
UKOW01f2237101017
310757UK00006B/425/P